Devilfish

Devilfish

poems by
Gaylord
Brewer

Red Hen Press Los Angeles 1999

Devilfish

Copyright © 1999 by Gaylord Brewer
All Rights Reserved

No part of this book may be used or reproduced in any manner whatever without the prior written permission of both the publisher and the copyright owner.

Published by Red Hen Press
P.O. Box 902582
Palmdale, CA 93590-2582

Cover art: "Once Upon the Beach"
   Oil on canvas
   50" x 45"
   © Mikhail Gubin, artist
   718·846·5708

Book and cover design by Mark E. Cull

ISBN 1-888996-15-3
Library of Congress Catalog Card Number: 99-63899

First Edition

and then there will be no more good, no more evil,
no more beyond good and no more beyond evil,
no more roses growing upside down in the dirt,
no more insects, and no more you and your rotten God.

—Alan Dugan

Contents

I

You Have Only What Remains	13
Carve Me in Wood	14
Still Life with Movement	16
Don't Touch Me	18
Cemetery Flowers	20
Night of Moment	21
A Note to the Watcher	22
Gloss Notes on a Kitchen Scene	24
Changing the Way You Eat	26
The Writers' Block	28
Dead Parent Poems	30
Dream	31
Fat Man Dying	32
The Night Bird	33
Black Billy	34

II

Everybody Loves the Devil	39
Vampire Western	40
Gorging a Forgotten Fury	42
Writing about Dogs	43
Sightings	44
Owl	45
Before the Welcoming Dinner	46
The Montgomery Clift School	47
Love Poem for Bears	49
A Little Sex Poem	50
The Man Who's a Genius in Bed	51
The Losers' History Book	52
The King of Trash	53
Years in the Wilderness	56
The Last	57

III

The Age of Good Barbarism	61
City of Rooks	62
Silence and Shadow	63
La Noche	65
The Burden of Fossils	66
The Burden of Fossils II	68
The Burden of Fossils III	69
Horns Forward	70
A Brief Hemingway Encounter	72
What the Meek Inherit	73
A Woman in the Theatre	74
Morning Verses	76
The Community Prospers	79
A Sunday Killing	80
Bones	81

IV

Greeting the Millennium Poem	85
Report from the Frontier	86
Emmitt	87
All You Need for Painting	88
Quotations on the Romantic Escape	89
Poem Written with One Hand Behind My Back	90
Keys to Drunk Driving	91
Before the Devil Knows You're Dead	92
Dr. Terror's House of Horrors	93
Dead Man's Chest	94
Heat Stroke	95
Morning with Goats	96
Message to Barleycorn	97
Aubade	98
After Stealing a Gerbera Daisy	99

Devilfish

I

You are the slayer of the man whose slayer you seek.

—Sophocles

You Have Only What Remains

Raise a window to begin, breathe in January,
feel it like smoke on the skin of your arms

When the church bell starts its cadence, low
and ominous, label the sound without prophecy,
continue counting until others lose interest

Think then of coming snows, of heaviness,
plan to search for that plastic shovel to dig
a way out later, to check and recheck
provisions, to watch the dog breathing
by the fire, to find a dog, to make a fire

Consider the bell persisting, forty chimes
at least, and do not believe it signals
a forgotten thing, do not tolerate indulgence

Say in a steady voice, today will pass as
yesterday has, in the tired manner of history

You take this too intimately, the opaque sky,
torn screen, sudden movement of leaves

Recall a single mockingbird, then another,
on the highest branches of a holly bush,
recall how the branches bent with red berries
and the berries seemed almost beautiful

Carve Me in Wood

The ribcage, freed from its fleshy constraint, should curve
invitingly, like bars an infant takes in its hands without thinking.
A tantalizing, even succulent arc, as if it had a rib to spare.

Make the breastbone of a simple white wood, soft on the surface,
relinquishing to the dullest blade or even a fingernail
but harder inside than one imagines. You'll get a longer burn
that way, slow heat. Still, the breast should make one think
of whales, silent ocean floors, an apple grove in moonlight.
Make it smooth on the ends, like a riddle waiting to be touched.

Some parts need your discretion, others merely kindness.
Legbones are standard walking sticks, armbones a hunter's arrows.
Fingers knotted toothpicks. The pelvis, a bowl for pears and grapes.
Please be generous with the cock and consider it a bone.
It deserves more artistry than it got, a straight piece of hickory,
not some leftover root just as easily made a big toe.

The pile of smaller bones should ignite easily, it usually does,
and soon will make curious music like a flag flapping in the desert.
Now is your time to relax, to enjoy some well-earned compensation.
But between chapters, as you finish the last drops of tea
and begin to ponder the relative morality of an afternoon nap,
periodically add the back and shoulders, the hipbone, the thigh.
I'll object only with an erratic pop and a tinkle of embers.

Before you doze off, position the skull in its proper place
on top. At first it may merely sizzle, its last claim a damp one.
But note, then, how it begins to catch on, how the eyes
you chopped blaze like a happy goblin, how the mouthhole
tries to lick you with a hot kiss for your efforts, how the top
of the head sputters and smokes in a furious final formulation.
A blistering thought laps upward even as the rest blackens.

You'll awake to a small but nice bank of coals. You can streak
your face with these, or dump them under the rosebush, or start
chopping more wood. For what difference to me then?

Still Life with Movement

A pear, representing innocence,
lies beside a peach, sensuality.
The pieces are equally voluptuous

in form and color, are rendered
in miniature to heighten
their effect. The knife, the scarred

table, these too may be important,
then abruptly all analysis
is interrupted by a child's hand.

The boy fingers the seductive crease
of the peach, the pear's
suggestive contour and coldness.

In his presence the fruit seems
a natural size. Our original
composition is destroyed forever.

Look how even the light bends
differently since this intrusion.
He thumbs the edge of the knife,

presses it into the table top.
Perhaps the boy represents texture,
how things feel on skin.

Perhaps a theme of impatience.
Surely, his mouth waters
in anticipation of the sweet syrup.

Consider his dreamy expression
which defies certain interpretation.
He replaces the knife, touches

the pear, the peach again, as if
deciding which to give his mother,
which to take first for himself.

Don't Touch Me

Your fingernails will ignite a fire.
They would scald my back, my chest, my face.
Look at me if you can't help yourself,
then keep a healthy distance for us both.

I don't eat. I taste copper on my lips,
and salt, and sometimes blood. My stomach
twists like a torch. Everything burns.
I've lost forty pounds in fifty-seven days.

Don't feed the animal. I've given up juice,
tomatoes, those creamy soups.
I drink broth for my partner's sake.
Light a cigarette, fill it all with smoke.

The best thing is to lie in bed,
back to the window. One pillow doubled
under the head, another clutched in the arms.
I don't talk on the phone. Don't call me.

Maybe you've heard that your body no longer
seems like your own. When it lets me
I make a few words on a notepad. I listen
to church bells, birds, cars, the rain.

It's April already. Where is spring?
My partner says the tulips aren't budding.
I have no time to water or cultivate,
no time for secrets. We've loved living here.

This could be my last effort. Don't say
what it means to you or pretend to be moved
toward a new life. None of that matters.
When you read this I'll be gone regardless.

Cemetery Flowers

The dead neither need nor desire them, nor care
for such displays. To the dead, cold under a hill
of clay and stone, the lavender of the wild iris
is no different than, say, an airless inky black
filling a box in a pit. The ripe and fragrant tulip,
the blood red rose drooping already on its thorns,
the angel's breath blown in broken swirls
over rectangles of sod, all less than worthless.

Help yourself. To mum and pansy, columbine
and calla lily. To dianthus and dahlia, taking
a daisy, too, to slip behind your lover's ear
as you make an offering of this sensuous buffet.
Be brave, collect the freshest only, ignore the dumb
etiquette of the living. It's a sunny afternoon,
it's May, see now how her hair swings softly as thin
hands reach for the blossoms. How white her skin

as your fingertips trace the fine high cheekbones
pulled to a smile, as in their sockets your eyes shine.

Night of Moment

This, the self-definitive night you've waited for,
the night you've dreaded with a sweet anxiety.
Imagine it so. Imagine that she comes
to you with her eyes like ocean diamonds,
the one who appreciates your incomplete perfection.
That sense of otherness beyond the explicable,
the swirling soothe of *now,* your quiet hand
riding on a thigh as smooth and white
as the last road to heaven. As the story proceeds

a gun is involved, an understated pledge,
that something arriving in you for a long time.
There's a hotel room, the sun through winter trees,
a pleasant dizziness of certain surrender.
This is the night you've dreaded and revered.
What will you do now, in this romantic interruption
of that fake *other* life? Money on the bed,
the cool cold fatedness, her curling laughter
which seems so simply distant you cannot answer.

A Note to the Watcher

Fragmentary to start. Perhaps a cry for help.
Perhaps a clutter of boys staring silently.
At some point a young woman, blonde, striking

hard at an arm grasping through a car window.
She is choking out words, is fearful, enraged.
Of course there are reasons why you hesitated—

the paralyzing shock of sudden violence, the heavy
traffic at the intersection, those were parts of it,
and of course you were drunk. The strayed

always deserve more forgiveness than they get.
And the boys, were you intoxicated by their casualness?
Her fists struck, her hair jostled, she wore a dress.

The car was green, full of dark shapes, men.
Did you actually lean on the pier and look away?
When you finally turned again in her direction,

hot with determination, was this supposed to impress?
By now a silver-haired man had arrived at her side,
thank god, and remember as you stood immobile

at the curb how he took her by the shoulders
and forced her onto the seat? Couldn't she have run
at any time? Wasn't she probably a whore? Or merely

young and stupid? And was that really you I saw
indistinguishable from the rest as the car sped away?
If it was, you should be ashamed, and I hope

you like the taste of it. Well, you can't go back.
You can't help now. And your resolve for next time,
wherever she is, isn't worth a goddamn to her.

Gloss Notes on a Kitchen Scene

—after Raymond Carver

The slits in the crust
normal enough in another context
here indicate lacerations.
Ditto for burned sugar:

Bruises. And steam rising
from the cuts, this is a woman's
helpless anger. The situation
we know is a hot one.

Therefore we know the woman
in other ways. Her simple act
of baking we find excruciating.
Her black sunglasses

do not indicate blindness.
Nor addiction. You could argue
sensitivity to light, yes.
But hiding eyes

we can only imagine. Her father
meanwhile silent at the table
blows on a bite, forks it in
like the moment's inevitability.

He's taking this one piece
at a time. His resignation
hints at familiarity. Why do we
assume the parent is the father?

The pathos of his silent
answer. This is hard for him
to swallow. Love makes it worse.
His for her, hers for some other.

Winter morning whips the house.
Wind speaks for itself.
Sunlight, its comfortless vision
supplies a final irony.

Bitter apples. Sugar, spice.

Changing the Way You Eat

Hold the salt, we're not killing
zombies here. No more encrusting
that steak as if it were a corpse in the cellar.

In fact, no more steaks at all. No t-bones
or porterhouses, ribeyes, sirloins, or strips.
Think about the color red
and the way your heart has struggled lately.
We'll get back to that.

When you need a sweet-salt
bitterness, take a lick off the arm.
That's where your life is, what's left,
layered there in the skin
like a woman's wet flower.

Sugar is not so bad as they report
but not so good either. Even ants won't
touch it. You might as well be chewing dirt
in the cemetery kitchen.

The coffee, wine, gin, that's another matter
entirely. The old liquid diet.
You'll drink your dinner once too often.

Of course, the late night habit is worst.
What happens when everyone,
maybe, is asleep. After the lights blink out.
Then the pillow is hot, your body moans
in odd places and the mind wanders
where it shouldn't. That's the eating that kills.
Cut that out and you've solved half
your problem. And this time, *mean* it.

The Writers' Block

He brings them in, as requested, in leg irons, chained
ankle to ankle. A few keep their heads lowered,
others peer bright-eyed at the dingy interiors,
one old geezer fakes a limp. Each, however, carries
a secret smile. For isn't this what they've deserved?

Didn't they always know that punishment was around
the corner? And what cage may contain the human spirit?
The guard has heard it all a hundred times before.
He wearily takes a key from his belt. The shackles,
eaten with rust, clang to the floor at a touch.

A little bark, a very little bite, that was the routine.
What a man had to do to make a living in the world.
He grabs a big woman in a chiffon blouse, squeezes
her into a cell as if he were wrestling tapioca pudding.
Five pages of historical romance by morning, if you

expect your yard time. She sucks in air; her face glows.
He touches a skinny free-verse poet on the back, the boy
stumbles, mumbling curses and squinting for his glasses.
Forty lines by lights out, punk. Any more mouth it's three
days of villanelles in the Pit. The kid snarls.

On and on down the corridor the guard locks them away.
Italian translators, mothers whose children flew,
suffocated spouses, defrocked liberals, former athletes,
new formalists, vegetarians, creative essayists . . .
On and on. He sighs and offers a half-hearted turn

to the last cell on the block. They took to their
sentences like a mutt to a bone. The clackity-clack
had begun. Into the night now like bees buzzing a bush,
like a pimp with a pocket mirror, like . . . maybe he should
lock himself up. The sun-speckled web of dew, the city

tilting like a doomsday trumpet on an angel's harelip.
Jesus, didn't other men have homes, dinners, wives?
More arrived every day, typed confessions in hand,
short-termers all. Weren't they finally a soft
and silly bunch? Anxious to enter, anxious to leave.

Counting down the hours until they were ex-jailbirds.
Then how they would crow. Of cigarettes, solitude,
stoolies, bed bugs, the moon through a tiny window,
showers and bunkmates and oh that lousy guardsman.
Isn't it about survival after all? A pencil smuggled

into grub, in a cuff or a seam, the black tip flashing
and somebody who deserves it going down?
While the rest, as if nothing happened, pass folded
pages beneath trays of spring water and gruel,
each hoping to be dangerous, without the hard time?

Dead Parent Poems

They're nearly on a par with new baby
narratives, surpass in angst dead grandparents
by a mile. For earnestness they remain
unparalleled. For sincerity, drip crystal tears.

He goes first with the big "C" or she
surprises with a delicate heart, but each
passes too soon. It's always heavy irony—
the 50-year cruise next month, early retirement

a sudden mockery, time a thief to the one left
this eternity of protracted loneliness.
Intentions are good. The son or daughter
at the bedside rendering an appropriate Psalm,

often 139, and later there's the ugly
business of first holidays, all the first dates
in the year after passing. See there, a child
stepping in courageously to organize the estate,

to remind strangers of biscuit cutters,
sunburns, father's stubble, undercurrents
of bitterness to fortify sweet/sour regret.
Everybody—every living body—suffering hell,

nothing useful at all, really, to add.
Those who haven't written them yet—they will.
A first, then a second, perhaps a beautiful baby
between, but these verses don't ever

stop, ever. Glib or not. Not in this life.

Dream

I wait sick in bed
again, iced with sweat,
the pain returned

behind the ribs,
just below
and left of the heart.

I remember my own
death   I died young.
For a few seconds

I could be anywhere
or any age. An old man
seeing his future

passed in a memory.
When I untangle
and stand my foot gives

away, I fall
and keep falling.
My body seems immense.

In the morning silence
cuts deep into me.
Fear. More promises.

Fat Man Dying

A fat man dies in a room. He dies alone, of course,
piss stains on his pants, an empty bottle,
the telephone not ringing. Nobody cares less.

But to make it interesting, let's say his spirit
rises from that heap of disappointed blubber, rises
into the night as the shimmering contour of an eagle.

At the Stop N Go, a woman looks out at the moon.
Life's a mess, really it's a miracle the bastard's
gone. For a moment, she thinks she sees a flickering

in the sky, then she turns to ring up two six-packs,
tall. A kid in a Miami Heat cap hands her ID,
ten dollars, says nothing. His mind is in the stars.

He heads out to his Chevy long-bed—with new chrome
running boards paid for, fuck you—tosses the sack
onto his girlfriend's lap. Fuck her too. Seven months

and zero place to go from here. She almost asks
if he saw the moving light, but who needs more sarcasm?
He doesn't love her. Bright night tonight, he says,

let's get out and go somewhere. Shit yeah, she says.

The Night Bird

Why even first consider it would
come calling for you? The autistic hum
of a ceiling fan, breezes thick
through a screen, why not a whacked-out
summer bird who can't sleep?
It's welcome company, a song in the dark
as you squint out at skeletons of branches.
But its voices begin to disturb you—
grating phrases of the mockingbird,
naturally, but also mewing of the catbird,
squawk of a grackle, trill
of a dark-eyed junco, even raucous scream
of a red-shouldered hawk, and they
haven't lived around here for a long time.
Probably you have all
the notes wrong, but still that voice
seems not one bird but a dozen in succession,
and, as nights go, sounds become words.
Sometimes weepy, sometimes stoic you sit
in moonlight in the doorway
captive audience to your weird buddy's concert.
Naturally it speaks to you, to you alone
on the last night, the night you open
the door gently as a mouse as the shrill
chip of a house finch becomes another call,
a siren never heard till now
as its black wings come fast to envelop you.

Black Billy

1.

The children he works with, young people
who call themselves blessed name him Black Billy,
as right a reference as any. He enjoys
the attention, recognizes even as he denies
its sober truth. Black Billy. The distance between
the life in his head and the one in the world.
Every year the distance greater, or maybe furrier.
Fleshy walls of the mind, flabby failures
of the body. Hair in odd and fractious areas.
Billy tells the kids to forget it, go home, Merry
Christmas and all that shit, see you in three days.
Someone gives him a chocolate bell and the man
nearly weeps. At home, he tastes the bell.
It's literally lousy. A white worm tapers
across red foil and rolls onto the table.
Black Billy plays a nauseated home edition
of This is My Life, flushes the worm and the dinner.
Call it a year, call it history, call it over.

2.

Billy too has a family. A tough and thoughtful
father silenced by abrupt illness, a mother
who knows how to laugh but believes in
spirits. Holidays, now, are when he least enjoys
visiting. He watches his siblings, their spouses
and children, doesn't envy their lives or his.
He sees himself in reflection performing as cloud
bringer, as dark uncle, as eccentric goat.
Billy's role has merit, advantages he could
also live without. He arranges his small gifts
into a sack, bundles a few rags, looks forward
at least to the drive down. The cold air, music—
Bizet and Berlioz, *Tosca*. He'll sing until his voice
croaks, until his eyes are sponges. Once
into the hill country, mix Black Jack and ice
at seventy miles an hour on curves, watch for hawks,
feel as rapturous as any man in allowed in this
our only life, *Black Billy* words rushing behind him.

II

The last act is bloody, however fine the rest of the play.
They throw earth over your head and it is finished forever.

—Pascal

Everybody Loves the Devil

—for Jordan Petrou Griffith

You find him under a harvest moon, in a hemp
basket fighting the river by your parents' farm.
You're wet to the thighs as you raise him
in a rotted blanket, pink-faced and bawling
with a tiny smile behind the suffering. *He's mine,*
you scream, *I deserve him, I don't care.*

When he pukes apple pudding on your
shoulder, it's a prophecy of better times.
When he squeezes his eyes and bellows damnation,
that means *I know everything tomorrow brings.*
You coo, *Little Devil you're my darling,
the boys at school don't know nothing about where
I've been.* Mamma and Daddy raise hell
about the mystery father, but when baby spews
his stuff and dumps a stinking load of sin
they crumble like two who've refound the faith.

I remember them days, says Mamma. *Bastard's
kind of cute,* says Dada. Look how his eyes
glow and our angel girl shines like a new woman.
Everybody loves the Devil. Everybody.
We watch him grow and grow and grow.

Vampire Western

You notice yourself slinking past mirrors
like a bloodsucker in a lurid children's tale.
If only that were so, that you gave

no reflection. Only sometimes, wrestling a key
into a door or passing a closed window
in moonlight, you see the sad-eyed monster

of presence who skulks beside you.
Jowls, chin, nose, translucent but unmistakable.
You can't recall when he stopped smiling,

when teeth began dulling behind
a routine of petulance. And the eyes he used
to brag about, that glowed like the Devil's own

child. A dangerous face, he fancied,
a face at least destined for a post office wall.
But his bluff's called, a finger twitches

on a six-gun. No last bottle of redemption.
No sweet white neck, powdered and virginal.
This is not the figure you want

preserved in a sideshow as the century turns over.
But it's your face, so learn to die with it.
Where is the countenance that could burn a village?

Or melt the daughter while her daddy weeps?
Think about the Man Inside, held merely,
you reckon, in stupid mortal clay.   And anyway

as the box of native soil is discovered at sunrise
and the last good woman in town marries your brother,
you're above it all, you're really laughing.

Gorging a Forgotten Fury

Welcome the beast to your parlor. He will arrive
anyway. Feel warmth rise between your
calves. Even through a woolen skirt, you know
his fur. His sides heave. The joy of ascent
and attack. The blood joy. He explains nothing.

That he even comes to you is honor enough.
With a slight ferocity, pressure ribs between
your legs, capture at once what you otherwise deny.
This shames you and your heart echoes
a primitive rhythm. You long to explain the past,

to theorize. But the beast licks and grins, dark
eyes expectant always of the next offered pursuit.
You reach both hands beneath, out of sight,
feel the inhuman head, skull below softness,
ears erect, wetness edging blackened lips.

Where will this fable end? In a wooded cabin.
At a fiddle dance on the floor of a lighted forest.
On a red path in snow, whiskers heavy with ice.
A final feast of myth and annihilation. Offer
all that you have, explain nothing, serve him.

Writing about Dogs

Listen, there's nothing trite in
that love as it happens.
If you choose to write about
this subject, you'd best be good,
or you will butcher something
better than you are.

The white dog sits by my chair,
silent, his nose lowered.
He sniffs my thigh and licks.
The plush hair, white like cotton.
He pushes his head into my hand,
brown eyes half-closed.
The ears back. That simple.

Sightings

Our cars lined the valley road, nose
to rear, as the pale pure incandescence
of evening lit the mountains—
so old they were worn to hills—
ridges of timbered dark and atavistic
regret, the gold of the cove,
the smoky sloping blue as we

pulled onto grass and more
followed, this traffic in the wilderness
persisting, perverse but accountable—
what did we desire so?—fawns
in indistinct distance, wild turkeys
crossing the acres like a frantic black
punchline, but we wanted more,

needed more for pity's sake, ran
with videos, we had come great distances
for one sure sight of the beast,
a black cub frightened in a tree
as we left dogs in sedans
with windows up, here was the untamed
thing itself, the mother somewhere

furious, we craved her to burst among us,
lay open bone with claw, capture
that too on 3/4" cassette, Christ was this
our only chance, light failing
as the infant gripped the branch, did we
have the lens to handle it, the wildness
there before us and what it did next?

Owl

The tawny owl is enormous, its domains
extensive. The mistake one makes is to take
this too personally. The silhouette,
your torch won't clarify it, your aspirations
are insignificant. Think of harbingers of defeat
to hold you to the path. Beneath the cypress
a black shape taut, a spread of wings,

and nothing you can ever do or imagine
or give name to may alter its solitary dignity.

Before the Welcoming Dinner

An older man, in his sixties by now, stands
at a kitchen chopping block. He is skinning a portion
of meat to celebrate a son's visit, perhaps a ham or roast
but most likely a large fowl, a turkey or hen.

The younger man, the son, may sit nearby speaking
with his father, but probably he relaxes in another room
as he stares out the window at a field or lake.

The older man approaches, one hand protecting
a prime piece of the animal, the center of ham,
the tip of loin, the heart or liver of bird. The son
bends forward, takes the offering into his mouth.

He tastes briefly the other's fingers, greasy with fat,
then leans away eating, let's say, the heart.
The young man chews, slowly, the salty vital
as the older man returns to his carving.
They relish this, the rare part, while they can.

The Montgomery Clift School

He has studied tilting the head
to catch those phantoms in the distance,
with eyes that can only be described
as soulful. He has devoted twenty years
to the art of leaning pensively
with one foot hooked over the other
or planted backwards with a leg bent.
How to cup a cigarette in the palm as if
he held the secret. Inside a party
carries on. Shouts, broken glass,
forced laughter interrupt his solitude.

Only seldom, however, does a beautiful
woman separate herself from the crowd
to join him in the garden, feigning
at first a mild surprise at his presence.
There has been electricity between them
all evening. Now with his first words
he will say to her, *It must be tough
living with your daddy's millions.*
Or he begins, *I remember a moon like this,
the night my wife died.* Or perhaps
the woman speaks first: *You don't care
for my friends, do you?* He answers
with smoke. There's going to be trouble.

However, this scene seldom occurs.
Actually, never. Performance has
become identity, a wall bracing a wall.
During the day he looks sideways at faces.
Was X perusing Y? Did Z catch W
peeking back? No. See how she scurries
for her appointment, how he gazes up
at the city clock and compares it
to his watch. What choice but espionage?

Better to take the elbow in the ribs,
the shopping bag in the thigh and feel
grateful. He crosses at the red, anxious
for a next cigarette in moonlight.
The early bird gets the worm, the worm
gets everybody. He must have a page
of dialogue, at least, ready and waiting.

Love Poem for Bears

—for C.

I growl myself awake at dawn, get aroused, pad out
for a big breakfast of nuts, berries, fruit, trout, salmon, eggs,
porridge for old times' sake. Then it's back to the cave.

I stoke a blazing fire, open and close books, blink
at walls, scratch my hairy neck. I'm not in a circus, no one
burns my feet to make me dance. The hunter hasn't come, yet.

Then it's time for a snooze until I will roar out for a big
lunch of nuts and berries, fruit, salmon and trout, eggs.
I turn my fuzzy back to the day, pull up a blanket, give the log

a poke. Speaking of which: I take my big bear prick
in one paw, curl the other under my snout like a pillow
for dreams of you: that's right, you.

A Little Sex Poem

The serpent's fat tongue
tipples at the ashen bud of her
forbidden rose.

The serpent cannot believe
his good fortune.

He gambols like a garter.
He plunders like a python.
Christ, how he *loves* being a snake
in her grass!

The Man Who's a Genius in Bed

His best creative work he does there, the girl
in the front row, a former butch colleague,
those young ladies from the optometrist's

office, he has them all, fills to drowning
their craving and luxurious shells,
manhandles, talks roughly and if they don't

like it they learn to like it, come
back for more whenever he demands,
women addicted not only to his delicious body,

but, poor things, his sadness, wit, intellect.
He sometimes whispers to the damp recesses
whole lines of startling verse, snippets

of song *recitativo,* those languages
forgotten beneath the din of vertical life.
Then, squinting at a dark ceiling, he gets

brutal, just a little, enough to slaughter
one on the altar of propriety. He does them
good, these ghosts, until a moment when, spent

and clammy, a banal gray ocean of thought
rippling under a voice not disgust, not
resignation, but familiar enough, he hears,

"Get up, idiot. Get up, walk into the world.
What if God is watching? Or, your Mother?"

The Losers' History Book

This will be a short book.
Life in the valley was—why not say it?—beautiful.
We awoke anxious to begin another day.
The sun shone through purple phlox. Can you imagine?
We were farmers, mostly. We loved our animals.
We loved our families. We had eleven words
for what you call soil, nine for the color green.
Winters were short. We planted, we sang, we drank
the local brew, made happy love to our wives.
Our children grew up healthy and knowing how to laugh.

Once, for several days, the crows were raucous.
Then silent.

When the Kaiser brought his guns over the mountain
we didn't have a clue. Good-bye, dear valley.

The King of Trash

One Tuesday morning, face up
in the dark you hear a city truck,
wheeze of hydraulic brakes,
whir of compactor, the shouts
of men holding with gloved hands
before leaping to curbs again.

As they pass without slowing, you
turn onto your stomach and pretend
to sleep. Your heart is loud,
your face hot. You've never felt
more alive. From this moment
you manage your debris. That good
relief each week as the bags
are taken anywhere not your home.
No more of that. No more cleansing
on someone else's account.

You shall wallow in a bed of trash.
But will the wife understand as
her vines are overcome?
That's her life out there too,
but she's never shared your sense
of culpability, of Big Picture and yes
of style, even when it stinks.

As weeks go by strays
don't leave one bag unclawed,
a cryptogram of chicken bones,
shredded towels, rotted pears.
It's July, so maggots throw a picnic.
To hell with recycling,
each item's use ends here, today.
Cans, bottles, jugs—
a kingdom of empties.

The neighbors bitch, cameras roll,
your wife's at her mother's.
Her last damning word to reporters?
You can't remember. Who foresaw
that keeping a life together,
every bit to apprize and cultivate,
would raise such a storm? Granted,
it's a disgusting performance.
Chewing noises keep the whole
street awake. Flies grow so
arrogant even grackles hurry south.
Your skin reddens with welts.
You smile and consider Job. Here,
you think, look at my life, nothing
is hidden, nothing denied.

Months ooze into fall and your
mountain rises, an art of squalor,
with a message you can bear it,
every discarded beginning, every
expiration, a stench reminding
of potpourri and lavender
as your mind spins giddily under
the notion of this seething garden,
and you climb sinking to the thighs
in a filthy stew of life, determined
to reach the top, to announce
yourself lord as you survey the rich
compost of your dreams.

Years in the Wilderness

Thirst wanted more than rain, stomachs more
than droppings from heaven. Debt and dependence,
the daily bread and water
of slaves. Now with no shelter, without even
a dream of freedom, feverish and dying
we ached for the old ways, the whip, the terrible
certainties. Monuments to gods
of men, crafted on men's bones. Bricks for Pharaoh.

We craved the golden rain, to drink and bathe
in liquid hot enough to scald.
In mountain shadow, in thunder, we erected
the beautiful Beast.
We danced in flames, sacrificed our shining bodies.
Here was paradise, now, in this world.
Like all things flesh, we yearned not for freedom
but for frenzy. Enough years slaughtered.

On the precipice a robed figure, its beard angry
in unnatural wind. *In its arms, stones.*

The Last

On the last evening of the earth
the rain stopped. For weeks it had bleached
roofs to gray. The wind thrashed
the last limbs, and the saturated birds,
all black, cackled in disharmony.
Then the wind, the way wind works, exhaled.

And finally rain again—eponymous, perfect,
imperturbable. Dark fell like a web.
Dark fell like veils. Like that, we were through.

III

. . . something always moving, and a name that does not come clear.

—Neruda

The Age of Good Barbarism

During this time the mountains, char slag
of ore and granite, become faces—
stretched mouths, burned and blinded eyes,
rock caught in a still scream.
The sky unrelenting beneath night's magenta,
ascending always to the chartreuse

of a next dateless dawn. Hide-warm shapes
arise then, bark to their god Retribution,
sift wreckage for any useful
edge. Iron, glass, a sliver of bone.
So much twists unwritten, forgotten, buried.
These are rich times, times prophesied,

when you take which mate you can
and eat the blood-sweet meat of the world,
when kings preside at stone tables
and the fat belly of the Crown
is carved and served as ceremony allows.
Now we begin again, create order anew again.

City of Rooks

For weeks I've perched beside the fire,
paced the drive, stopped each time inside the gate.
I lose count at seventy nests, begin again,
am lost again. My shoes are caked with excrement
and still birds circle the ragged branches of their city.

I tell you, I've tried to translate the language
of a rookery, and my failure I dedicate to you.
Their unbeautiful caws over the brae, black formations
in the sky as emblems of dispatch. Their arrogant strolls.
I'm sorry. But believe me, that world is coming.
Rooks and jackdaws will breed on our walls,
the ravens return with magnificent indifference.

Silence and Shadow

I Silence

If truth were told, you grow
stronger spending your days in it.
Your movements a survey
of a world's end, your life a mere
scripture of patience. Let us wait and see.
An Irish family fidgets for a bus
down the mountain. The girl removes
a plastic bull from her purse. How white
her father's legs are! You appear
without sound or gesture, without
even a hat. Clouds wake up grumbling.
A table of American teens glances at
the sky, laughter split by wind.
Voices lower. A red-faced Welshman
speaks to fill the sudden gap,
he knew the famous director, he did . . .
The rains start for the first time in a
month, but even the needful know better.

II Shadow

The late sun dropped a shadow across
sand and into breaking water.
The shadow contained its body,
the body existed fully only in shadow.
So they say. All you know for sure
is that you are taller than the sea, even
than drifts of polished stones.
You could reach to the waves
and fill the boat of every fisherman in
Garrucha, could bind their salty hearts.
They say no sharks swim this ocean.
You could bring them here.

At night you dream of midget bulls,
flat-headed, afraid. They are all
there is now and don't want the sword.
You lift them by pitiful horns,
hide a freckle-faced one under your
couch, another in the children's room.
The matadors come anyway. The bulls
die. You wake, irritated by light
from a neighbor's balcony. But when you
look the light is the moon, the moon,
shadow. Even if you chose to speak
it wouldn't answer, and that's the point.

La Noche

Imagine that Garrucha
smoldered like a lost city
between the
mountains that
defined her, imagine
the mountains were black
ramparts. Would you rest
your forehead,
hope the wind sufficient
to keep flies off skin?
It never is.
Imagine that the
garden flowers, so cared
for, surrendered
color for an off-hand
shade of *who can say?*
Imagine that every
life arrived here.
Would you succumb to
such dry, indifferent kisses?
What if the peaks of
the mountains,
the glow between them
on the shore, were a
proposition of clarity?
Now imagine an
animal you have never
known, coughing
its plaintive response
for hours
across the desert valley.
And then what happens?

The Burden of Fossils

So you require to be a relic of
the earth? Your actions suggest so.
The first shower this week,
the smoothed hair, that last clean
shirt. The steep walk to Mojácar
pueblo as usual. Head down,
heaving strides, sweat and blood.
Whew. But a few cool minutes

on the village square bring you
together. As you study the
Andalucían landscape—receding
mountains ahead, sea to the right—
the men begin their afternoon.
A single pair, then another, then
clumps splitting and regrouping
like atoms. *Calmete*. It's not your

time yet. Soon the women arrive
in their dresses, the square fills
with quiet anticipation. Still you wait.
Your finest quality is endurance,
so quit pacing. The Spaniards
break, return to couples, split
again and go. The next Saturday
they return. You get comfortable.

After a few months your shirt
doesn't look so nice, your nails
curl into obscene question marks.
In a year skin drips from the face,
revealing a lurid grin. Too much
sun will do that. Then the old man
is sent in, bends with a grunt—
Jesus, so much garlic with lunch . . .

*when will he get **his** final rest?*—
tosses your bits into the truck.
And as you slide off with the load,
your sudden irrational dread is that
this is not the archeology site.
That peculiar smell. But you go
with your smile, wave adiós as a
finger cracks off. Back in the hole.

The Burden of Fossils II

And the next day was worse. Wind boomed outside
like artillery, tables and chairs sprawled into groves.
Almond trees bent like sticks. Below a swirling viaduct,
the men retired to their heavy trucks to smoke.
Every spade the gardener raised came down empty.

An elemental battle was being fought, one you're wiser
out of. In 1966, an American B-52 lost four hydrogen
bombs in the fields of Palomares. It's easy to be
dramatic in the desert. To use a phrase like *doomsday
wind*. The pants on the clothesline were a twisted mess.

A student archeologist from Granada huddled in the
pit with her young professor. It's lonely digging the past,
where you have to scream to hear yourself whisper.

At this rate, their findings would return to the earth
by evening, careful labels erased like waves over
a name carved in sand. Arms and faces covered gray,
their legs, their lips, their eyes, sealed forever in
that first dry embrace. It's hard work, and you eat late.
Lanterns swing. The sky explodes and dust answers.

The Burden of Fossils III

Before they finished dinner, without
coffee, everyone went out to look at the bowl.
It was after nine o'clock.
One archeologist was still sweeping, chipping,
sweeping, chipping. They leaned over for a peek.
The red clay bowl sat tilted, half uncovered,
like a dusty casserole dish held in rock.
The woman working smiled up out of the hole.
She wiped her forehead with a dirty arm.

The bowl was at least three thousand years
old, and the woman attractive,
rumored as junior faculty from the Universidad
de Almería. This was a sure tenure-maker.
She smiled again, self-conscious about
appearance. The bowl waited nearby, destined
for a museum, a glass shelf, an explanation card.
Everyone shared the fragile moment. One errant
hammer tap could ruin it all.

Coffee gurgled. They went in for tarts and flan.
There was much general discussion
and excitement. Here was something different—
going outside, the woman speaking to them,
of course the bowl itself, and no one even thought
to suggest the earth be left to the earth, that
the extraction of a bowl contained its tiny tragedy,
or that the future could best be revealed
anywhere but in a violated past.

Horns Forward

Notice the legs of the chair thrust upward
at the school desk, as if horns in attack,
pointed threats like the *now* of Lorca's dream.
That's the language he was raised with.
The boy knows the romance of bulls and art.

He has studied the Bronze Age sculptures,
the Picasso sketches. They concur that
the modern world begins as Pedro Romero
saves an aristocrat fallen from horseback,
distracts the bull with his own hat.

Or perhaps it was Romero's grandfather who
ushered an era in on foot. Well, stories
differ, but so does truth from what is needed.
The boy knows of Romero's greatness.
Killing six thousand bulls without a scar,

his death at 84 in his birthplace of Ronda,
which boasts the world's most ancient ring.
An arena of stone. The frown of Belmonte,
the long-limbed grace of Joselito,
the return at sixty of that national rogue

El Cordobés. He has learned. Veronica,
media veronica, breast pass. Puntilla, a dagger
stabbed into the bull's head when he refuses
to die, sits with a black tongue out,
pissing himself, shiny in his own blood.

He knows a country so enamored of *duende*,
a term he comprehends only by sound,
that no one separates the real from the dance.
He knows this last especially, sometimes feels
he has lived his whole life that way.

The fear in his heart he doesn't speak of.
Unable to divide instructed passions—
horns attacking, photos of victory or shame,
the arc of a human scream—from a submerged
reverence for life. *Six thousand bulls.*

A Brief Hemingway Encounter

He is rarely sighted in these remoter parts, and honestly
I have been relieved. So a gray afternoon at the beach,
siesta sacrificed for cold feet, was the last thing
I thought would interest him.
When the bus to the mountains finally arrived,
I saw immediately the hazy, familiar profile already boarded.
Believe me, you would have recognized him.
Heavy body stuffed uncomfortably onto a cushion,
skin red and tough, squint as handsome as Gable's.
With a single word of encouragement, or a nod,

I was ready to supply the material and take my punishment.
How about this month spent in the "Lorca Room"?
My behavior around the other artists, the English expatriates
and their lonely wives? Even, why not, that I've given
up trying to get properly drunk in Spain? I don't have
the something for it. But I'm writing his lines,
because the old man doesn't acknowledge me,
just stares out the window. He's fading already.
The bus curves toward Simon's bar. The men have finished
tying palm branches into canopies over trucks,

are decorating the beds with flowers. Tomorrow morning,
Sunday, a procession concludes the Fiesta de San Isidro.
I turn for an indication of what we think of it—
native ritual, or sham tourism needing to be gutted?
But he's almost gone, and I can't help a quick breath:
He doesn't look at me because he doesn't know I'm there.
And as the body disintegrates, I see in an old man's pudgy face
the saddest, clearest eyes I've ever seen, eyes oblivious
to the village, suited only for the dead. He wants to join them.
I went as far as I could and didn't quit. Don't look at me.

What the Meek Inherit

The earth, brother
the earth shall be theirs

The parched lands
and leaden, lifeless seas

The derision of the ones
who gave it to them

A Woman in the Theatre

The real drama involved angel-blonde hair
looped behind an ear. A mouth slowly chewing.
One leg across the other, taking turns on top.
The excruciating shape of a thigh in striped pants.
Nose, cheek, hands, on and on maddeningly.
Your view from the row behind took imagination—
an inconspicuous slump, eyes holding their gaze
stage left until they watered, then holding more.
Surely she was the partner of the dark lead actor,
the student-lover of the arrogant director?
You lick her downy stomach, taste the neck,
ask her, to your surprise, to marry you tonight.

It seems right in the setting, why bother with guilt?
Then the show's over. She puts on her coat,
leaves immediately. By managing your pace
you arrive in the parking lot behind her,
fake a yawn, stretch, gain more seconds to suffer.
Her hair seems, this is no joke, to contain light.
The light goes. You fold into the passenger's seat.
Was there a story, an excuse, a slim probability
as she stood on the walk in a green coat,
poised to step into the night and out of your life
forever? Don't play the fool more than you need to.

Then it's morning. You watch a mockingbird poke
for seed. It finds the feeder empty, abandons
a bare limb. You begin to search for a true
subject beneath the apparent one. Something about
opportunities, hard choices, moments of grace
that, if forsaken, carry their bounty elsewhere.
Or perhaps a lesson in common foolishness, romantic
idiocy, not knowing what you have until it's gone,
et cetera. Or perhaps the true subject is neither
of these, but merely a reminder of our incomplete
time on this swirling planet, of the longing
for that other who might repair our imperfect love.

Morning Verses

Her red poppies quiver
in their jar, as if frightened,
as she was yesterday
risking fence and field.
She had had to have them,
their petals were tissue.

The girl wears a yellow
blouse. She hurries to
compose words, hurries
before a knock on the door.
The birds temporarily
are silent. A bell clangs in
the valley. How many days
remain? How many
before she sees her friends,
they share her stories?

Outside the window her
mother walks in the garden
carrying a basket.

She brushes the poppies
with her fingertips.
Even her delicate hands
cannot feel the petals,
they are too light to exist.

A black cat circles the house.
Her store of bad luck
has turned so inward, she

scratches away her own hair.
In a shape signifying what?
The cat could be herself.

She hears her father's
falling easel, hears a ripping
canvas, his curses. For her
the mountains opened.
They invited her to see them.
She tastes the cigar in
his mouth, his Cuban
breakfast, strings and ashes.

Yesterday she petted the
dog, against all good advice.
What a lonely little animal!
She saw the blood ticks
gorging inside its curved ear.
Here was a real lesson,
a lesson of life. Her hand
on its warm belly, grazing
between rows of purple teats.

Empty chairs surround a table
beside fig and olive trees.
Perhaps a party will take
place, perhaps already has,
each boy traveling
alone for a single chance
at her company. She agrees
to meet them only as a group.

Beneath her room, the sisters
who clean the house
prepare today's meals,
which her mother will praise.
Muffled voices could be
laughter, the women joking
of their husbands, of the night
before, of what great and
needy gentlemen they became
after the wine was served.

The girl closes the volume
of private verses, presses
a hand onto skin.
Her palm feels cold, her
chest hot. She is irritated by
the fear of interruption.
All this time to herself, and
no solitude. Look at the sky!
What would she do today?
It was too gray to walk
the beach. Deep in the house,
a door closes. She hears
footsteps. She yearns for
them to turn in her direction.

The Community Prospers

What a sound of crying from the carts
on the road to Pueblo Nuevo!

—Antonio Machado

Corpses of timber in unremarked pyres
like splintered ribs of ships.
Dozers, gorged and sodden beneath a slate
sky. They are monsters, not symbols
of monsters. No boundary
except the one approaching, slab locked
into slab across surrendered earth.

A last mosaic, signed with our black name.

A Sunday Killing

The neighbor dog, sad and lonely bitch, dropped
the baby bird from her mouth running. I had seen her
tense, and jump, and I shouted and rushed for
the adjoining yard—fuck their rudeness and Christianity—
carried the robin back, unfolding each wing,
turning each, checking the legs. It opened a yellow
beak, silently, instinct requiring a portion.

I put it inside our fence for the mother
to claim. When I returned from the grocer,
I rechecked the yard before letting our dog out.
Listen to me: it lay there in the same spot, no longer
a bird, just downy lightness and guts, the head cleanly
missing. Dark clots on feather.
I held it, the thing that had been alive and wanting.

I got the stink of its deadness on my fingers, pulled
each wing, watched each fall limply back. What
had done this? There are no cats here. A squirrel, *this*?
Why hadn't the mother returned?
And what had I done, was I responsible, with chicken
in a sack ready for carving? The head alone
taken as a trophy, one could only hope suddenly.

This is the hell we live and die in, *this* world. You
who pass my house, well-dressed and sated with worship,
with grievances and petty revisions, hurtful
acts of goodness, we are killers, each of us,
me especially and you most of all,
with no condolence except we'll burn, believe that.
Open your prayerful eyes. We're burning now.

Bones

Crush them on a Lake of Mourning, to shimmy
in glints and splinters over earth's
bed, boiling finally to an appropriate broth.
Try bathing in this.

Reserve skulls to rope for lanterns
through the village's fiesta. Light the mouths
with candles until their hinged laughter
stinks like soap.

Do as you desire. Bones take care of bones.

IV

*—Nothing happens? Or has everything happened,
and we are standing now, quietly, in the new life?*

—Jiménez

Greeting the Millennium Poem

Same bleached sky, scrubby tree-claws.
The river's same stillness.
Over all a sheen, somehow, of the absolute.
It is late, nearly noon, when life yawns
again inside houses. A slippered foot
inching between bottles.
Stains on a couch, a torn curtain.
A head as brutal as a pomegranate.

One door opens, one closes, in the village.
Cold slapping silly, forsaken bodies.
A hand on a forehead. *Day One, dear God.*
The sting of sulfur. Bleary landscapes.
As suddenly, on the river, a single blue heron
unfolds its aged awkwardness,
talons trail the slate surface
and a slow and terrible beauty rises.

Report from the Frontier

My life is going to change. I feel it.

—Raymond Carver

I am writing you again from the edge
of pale lands. Time has passed, I know.
I hope you haven't suffered much
are still alive and capable
of happiness. Perhaps only a lunatic

would choose this life. I wait,
study the horizon for what's not there.
When air is cold, I strip to shorts,
hunch silently until my skin hums.
When ground cracks with heat, I bundle

in furs and sweat away regret.
I think of you. I am sure you know
this and all is forgiven. Sure in my heart,
but my head rattles like a zoo of ghosts.
Day and night are the same,

time's glacier. Lately I can't distinguish
sleep from wakefulness. Don't worry.
When others arrive I'll be finished,
footprints and empty bottles
the sole relics of my lost discovery.

Emmitt

—for Vivian Shipley

He was one of Pirtle's brothers, older or younger
I'm not certain, they were all ancient to me.
He was the one who'd gone to Alaska decades earlier,
reasons forgotten, and stayed. I've no recollection
of his appearance, except perhaps he was a large man,
loud. A Handley. Once each year for many years
he visited Kentucky, an event, boarded with Momo,
whom he alone call *Agatha*, complaining

even in winter it was too hot for him down here,
that his blood had thickened. His departure, earlier
than scheduled, always attributed to January
or February heat waves. Some memory
of exotic foods, probably smoked salmon, something
of inflection and pitch of voice, almost a brogue.
Perhaps he drank. Possibly frequent toasts were raised.
May ye live as long as ye want to, want to long as ye live . . .

Our only conversation together concerned annual
invitations to visit, promises of Eskimo girls
available and willing. When he died, after Pirtle,
I suppose whoever cared for him up there, buried him there.

All You Need for Painting

Two flat-headed hog bristle brushes,
medium and wide, to sweep like brooms on fire.

One detail brush of pure Kolinsky sable,
Russian in design. This is your exotic child,
spend some money on her.

A family of misshapen colors in it together—
hot-tempered cadmium red; lemon yellow slipping
off a summer dress; the schemer cerulean blue.

Canvases to fasten your vision, cotton duck
primed for eternity. Various shapes for framing
the unruly compositions of the world.

Required extras—palette and knife, linseed oil,
a quantity of turpentine. Rags and more rags
for cleaning up messes or starting again.

An easel small enough to carry with you always.
A fool's fascination with light and form.

The hands of a midwife.
The habit of a buzzard.

A landscape to lunge into.

Quotations on the Romantic Escape

In his cell, Capone didn't once wish to die
on the street in a flag of bullets. He swallowed
bloody steak as the syphilis ripped
his body. Reportedly he would sometimes laugh
at the passing screws, "You clowns never learn."

✦

Gauguin populated the island with brown
children. They competed to bring the sweetest
mango, the most succulent guava. In a letter dated
April 17, he wrote: "I cannot paint the color
of sand. It seems this life, too, must be destroyed."

✦

Dean never married the starlets he escaped
with, horizon-bound, taillights red in a storm.
From the biography: "Name one of those honeys now.
It was a movie, in the morning they didn't
look so good to me. Neither did I."

✦

On his deathbed in satin sheets, Jefferson,
blind, surrounded by books, lowered his quill
to shape last words. A slave woman
of forty years cried as she held the dairy steady:
"That dream that must not die, has surely died."

Poem Written with One Hand Behind My Back

And I'm not as young as I was.
These gymnastics, believe me, exact a price,
but the old magic remains the best,
and as the expression goes
age and treachery will always beat
youth and enthusiasm.
You don't believe me?
Look, here, while you were looking elsewhere,
a flower, a dove, everything you ever wanted
blooming in the torrid night air.

Keys to Drunk Driving

Sometimes, with the sun pallid behind hills
of an unknown state, you will find yourself
driving straight into the arms of God.
That's number one. Number two, there are no
natural enemies on the road, except for cops.

The rest you learn as you go. How music,
right music, can steer you. Dvořák, Debussy,
pick your own accomplices. The gradations
of failing light. How to pour, steady
and inconspicuous, one-handed. How your mind

jangles like bones on a leash. Your face
in a freezing wind burning, your blood
a bandit framed with two sides open.
How you fly hot and deadly with your brothers,
soft in armor, inevitable, toward what's there—

Before the Devil Knows You're Dead

You approach congestion in the road,
blue sirens announcing Gabriel's Good Times.
Through the slot, catechismal nonsense—

pins and needles, camels, the shortest distance
to Katmandu. What's the difference?, you answer.
The doors open anyway—slow, gold, trumpets.

The keeper nods, bald as a plate.
It's cold here in a gown and underwear.
You're can't tell sky from sea, everybody grinning

like loons as they lean a harp in your direction.
The atmosphere is thin as clouds, as weak tea.
You click heels, wish for thirty minutes

earlier and a sticky back table at Nick's Hot Spot.
A confiding drink, the boys in crimson suits.
What did you ever do to damn yourself so?

Dr. Terror's House of Horrors

—for Ron Koertge

Or vice versa, phrases equally blood-chilling.
The point is, it's a coup for Amicus Films,
Christopher Lee and Peter Cushing
stolen for a one-picture deal. Those lurid pastels,
that wide screen. The pacing, flat as Iowa,
can't be resuscitated even by the best backdrop
of Bulgarian hill country or smoke-oily peasant

village. Finally, everyone's on the train.
Lee plays the doubting nerd, takes his paycheck
and lets Cushing run the table as Dr. Terror:
slouched hat, goat's beard, rolling eyes.
Fingers like sardonic, twisted sticks turning
each Tarot. The first young man
in the cabin, all right, he taps the deck

three times, he'll know his future, ha ha.
He shouldn't have. The future's bad: illicit
burial, bloodless woman, impolite secret that won't
shut up even under stone. The other men laugh,
smirk into rushing darkness. Lee pronounces
Terror a kook and pushes up his glasses.
Cushing smiles, his fingers a black basket.

Their long night ahead. Who shall be the next?
Shadows cross the laughter now, tension
stiffening each new suit. The young men, even young
Donald Sutherland, want their story. One by one,
mocking in turn, they've got to learn
if it's the leering skull on a mantle of roses
or the serpent, knowingly, over a prince's sword.

Dead Man's Chest

Drink, the Devil will do the rest.

At age nine, I cherished those tattered
killers stomping a crewmate's ribcage.
Assaulters' flesh sallow and flagging,

victim's lungs saltwater-full
or powder-scorched. Still, fifteen men
seemed excessive. They're glad he's gone,

greedy times, but this was overkill.
Oh sure, the chest might be of wood,
disclose sodden treasure bound

in leather and rusty hinges. Stones,
their weight deceptive, atop a rotted map.
"X" scrawled at the spot. But preferably

they flog some dead bastard
to pieces, laughing and disdainful,
eyes bobbing in a current of cheap rum,

Jolly Roger dancing on black
and I loved the rest of it, the tough
sauciness of surrender to worst impulses,

the ho ho ho, trusting the Devil to navigate.
Claiming our coin, a celebrated
camaraderie of betrayal, lust and song.

Heat Stroke

Finer evolutions of human kindness, no biting
and any response except a scowl, drip away
with the fantasy of a reasonable life celebrated
beside an ice cube ocean, with swizzle stick
diving boards, the frosty edge of a cocktail
tumbler as a children's slide, lemon twist surfboard
and an olive beach ball. Ow, watch your nose.
Nobody laughs
                because none of it happens, forget it.
This is August, when a lover's head's as ripe
as an ugly melon, when you roll in blackberry
thistle with your nakedness mumbling mad laughter,
fruit and blood the same on the skin
and a tick like a baseball careering off your neck
into clouds buttery with murder. The postman,
groping for his gun, fires only a limp cigarette.

Morning with Goats

The blue mug hovers beneath your nose,
tragic for an hour over the murder of coffee beans.
A big maple flutters fingers of innuendo.

Still, you find your shoes and step forward
to embrace the day. Ah yes, this is the new week.

Red potatoes, each preposterously unfunny,
rumble in your pocket and a purple lily blooms.

The white goat, the nice one raised by dogs
who likes his ass scratched, munches half a potato
and spits out the rest.
He rolls sexy eyes to indicate you are a fool,
returns to dreams of goat-love and fresh biscuits.

The other beast, the contrary one with no name,
butts toward a silo. He's either
playing a fun game or wants to kill you.

Stumbling back beneath a sheet of sunshine,
you are immediately accosted by kamikaze mosquitoes
in formation like a cartoon exclamation point.

As you wave wildly toward that first thirsty needle,
drooling with hate and desperate to be understood
by wealthy and big-boned women,
you discover two hard lumps just beginning
but already distinct on your forehead.

Behind the barn something guffaws. The moon
attacks, scimitar blazing, and morning is finished.

Message to Barleycorn

I need to see you tonight,
come like the photo we keep
of Jack London cocked
in a leather jacket—

hair, black tentacles,
eyes, closed switchblades.
John—handsome as the devil.
Come to my door like that,

a bruised aviator
with enough war in his pocket.
We won't discuss the enemy
or the lost brother.

Come with a shadow's intent.
We'll watch the sky rose
then darken, as goats bleat
in their private nightcomings.

Aubade

None of the feeling coalesces
until after our early walk.
Sun dazzling, preternaturally large.
Tulips already turn earth for it.
I spot a woodpecker,
a downy, high up on the hardwoods
where I've heard him working.

The dog looks at me
as if we are waiting for something.
I press in a few soft ridges
without malice. My part
in the mole drama. I'm glad he's back.
Call this false spring, if you must.
But these months I've not

known myself, have wanted no part
of the world. Two strong legs.
My breathing clear. The dog lunges,
ecstatic for a squirrel
he has no chance of.
And I, startled, realize I am grateful
to be part of it a while longer.

After Stealing a Gerbera Daisy
from the Gravesite
of an Eight-Year-Old Girl Buried Yesterday

I take the easy path
to redemption—
I plant
cucumbers, yellow peppers
early girl
tomatoes and squash.
I weed saplings
from the wildflower bed,
bury the bulb
of a honey dahlia,
replacement for a young
plant inexplicably broken.
It's hot work, soil
cakes my skin like black salt.
I don't use gloves
in the garden, not today.
I want my hands dirty.
I'm finished
with cemeteries for now.
Amanda, go peacefully
and dream no more.

Acknowledgements

Much of this collection was written during residencies at the Fundación Valparaíso (Almería, Spain), Hawthornden Castle (Midlothian, Scotland), and the Guest House at New Light Studios (Beloit, Wisconsin). Appreciation to my hosts and caretakers. Acknowledgments, also, to the editors of the publications where the following poems appeared:

The Alembic: "Horns Forward," "Morning Verses"; *Asheville Poetry Review*: "The Last," "You Have Only What Remains"; *Barkeater: the Adirondack Review*: "Sightings"; *Barnabe Mountain Review*: "The Burden of Fossils II"; *Birmingham Poetry Review*: "All you Need for Painting," "Morning with Goats"; *Blue Mesa Review*: "The Burden of Fossils III" (as "The Burden of Fossils IV"); *Chattahoochee Review*: "Love Poem for Bears"; *Chelsea*: "Carve Me in Wood," "Still Life with Movement," "The Writers' Block"; *Clackamas Literary Review*: "Bones"; *Connecticut Review*: "After Stealing a Gerbera Daisy," "The Night Bird"; *Crab Orchard Review*: "City of Rooks"; *Ellipsis*: "Don't Touch Me," "Gloss Notes on a Kitchen Scene,"; "Night of Moment," "Poem Written with One Hand Behind My Back," "Writing about Dogs"; *Fish Stories*: "Bones"; *Greensboro Review*: "Message to Barleycorn"; *Gulf Coast*: "The Montgomery Clift School"; *Liberty Hill Poetry Review*: "Silence and Shadow"; *Licking River Review*: "A Brief Hemingway Encounter"; *Linq* (Australia): "Heat Stroke"; *Main Street Journal* (England): "Vampire Western"; *New Letters*: "Before the Devil Knows You're Dead," "Everybody Loves the Devil"; *Oakland Review*: "Sightings"; *Orbis* (England): "You Have Only What Remains," "Don't Touch Me"; *Owen Wister Review*: "Dream"; *Pavement Saw*: "A Woman in the Theatre"; *Poet Lore*: "The Losers' History Book"; *Poetry Ireland Review*: "Cemetery Flowers"; *Poetry Nottingham International* (England): "Love Poem for Bears"; *Poetry Wales*: "Keys to Drunk Driving," "A Woman in the Theatre"; *Press*: "Before the Welcoming Dinner," "Owl"; *Quarterly West*: "Changing the Way You Eat"; *Red Rock Review*: "Dead Parent Poems"; *Reed Magazine*: "A Sunday Killing"; *Talking River Review*: "The Burden of Fossils"; *Treasure House*: "Vampire Western"; *Trestle Creek Review*: "The Man Who's a Genius in Bed"; *Voices West*: "Gorging a Forgotten

Fury"; *West Wind Review*: "Greeting the Millennium Poem," "The King of Trash"; *Whiskey Island Magazine:* "Fat Man Dying," "The King of Trash."

"You Have Only What Remains" won the 1996 Virginia Highlands Festival Contest, poetry division. "Don't Touch Me" was a prize winner in the 1996 Bridport Arts Centre Competition (Dorset, England) and was published in their anthology. "Everybody Loves the Devil" was reprinted in the anthology *Starting Rumors: America's Next Generation of Writers* (Grand Junction, Co: Pinyon Press, 1999). Some of these poems appeared in the chapbooks *Predator in the House*, winner of the 1996 Chatfield Software Chapbook Competition and published by North Star Press (Hiram, Ohio), and *The Age of Good Barbarism*, winner of the 1997 Palanquin Press Chapbook Contest (University of South Carolina, Aiken).

Thanks also to Claudia Barnett; Trish Domengeaux, Mikhail Gubin, Billy Renkl; and the Research Committee, English Department, Middle Tennessee State University.

Biographical Note

Gaylord Brewer is a native of Louisville, Kentucky. He has published nearly 400 individual poems, several chapbooks, and the full-length collection *Presently a Beast* (Coreopsis, 1996). He is also a prolific literary critic whose books include *David Mamet and Film* (McFarland, 1993) and *Charles Bukowski* (Twayne/Macmillan, 1997). Recently, he has held writing residencies at the N. A. L. L. Art Association and the Cave de Lesvault, both in France. He earned his Ph.D. from Ohio State University and is currently an associate professor at Middle Tennessee State University, where he edits *Poems & Plays*. He lives in a log house on a few acres in rural Tennessee.